To our dear
friends — forever
friends — forever! & thee ♡
memories of the sea ✳
Patti, Jack & Adam

FAMILY HOUSES
by the SEA

FAMILY HOUSES
by the SEA

ALEXANDRA D'ARNOUX
JÉRÔME DARBLAY

With the collaboration of Barbara Dixon
and Elisabeth Selse

Translated by Patricia Southgate

Clarkson Potter/Publishers
New York

Family Houses by the Sea
by Jerome Darblay and Alexandra d'Arnoux

Translation copyright © 1993 by Clarkson N. Potter, Inc.

Published by Clarkson N. Potter, Inc. 201 East 50th Street, New York,
New York, 10022. Member of the Crown Publishing Group.

Originally published in France by Editions E/P/A.
Copyright © 1992 by E/P/A, Paris.

Typographic design: Frauke Famira
Editor: Joëlle de Fouchier

Printed in Italy by Amilcare Pizzi SPA

CLARKSON N. POTTER, POTTER and colophon are trademarks of
Clarkson N. Potter, Inc.

Library of Congress Cataloging-in-Publication Data

Darblay, Jérôme
Family Houses by the Sea / by Jérôme Darblay
and Alexandra D'Arnoux.
p.   cm.
ISBN : 0-517-59165-0 $ 45.00
1. United States–Social life and customs – 1971 — 2. Dwellings–United
States. 3. Seaside architecture–United States. 4. Europe–Social life and
customs – 1945 — 5. Dwellings–Europe. 6. Seaside architecture–Europe. I.
D'Arnoux, Alexandra. II. Title.
E169.12.036 1992   92-16349
909'.0946–dc20   CIP

ISBN : 0-517-59165-0

10 9 8 7 6 5 4 3 2 1
First American Edition

CONTENTS

Houses in nature

Most of us have, stored away in some corner of our minds, the memory of a house by the sea. Maybe we were city children, but it was the country place that cast its spell. We left behind the city for a day, a week, a month, or, if we were very lucky, the entire summer. We ran along the beach searching for shells, scrambled over rocks, explored secret coves and fished off the pier. Our houses had wide wood floors and screen doors that banged, or docks out front with boats tied to them. We slept in tiny attic rooms, or tents pitched in the woods. Nature was all around us, in the dunes and in the starry nights. Returning to the city, we longed for the days of summer and the smell of the salty air and swore that, no matter what happened, we would always find our way back to the shore.

These memories inspire the places we are drawn to as adults. We crave the distances of beaches, the vastness of the sea, the microcosm of a shell collection. We dream about verandas and wicker furniture, bonfires and beach picnics, living in the great outdoors again. And whether on the shifting sands of Cap Ferret, the stark cliffs of the Isle of Wight, or a rocky island off the coast of Maine, we conspire in our dreams to recreate these memories for our children.

ATLANTIC CRUSOE

Above : On Cap Ferret, fishermen and oyster farmers have always lived in rustic cabins built rather haphazardly on the dune. Right : A siesta in a string hammock. Following double page : Nineteenth century rocking chair, stripes, provençal boutis, coverlet, and lots of blue furnishes the guest cabin.

rown as a berry, tousled mop of sun-bleached hair, bare feet dug into the sand, eyes squinting, dazzled by the reflection of the fish-silver sea—a boy, not very big, barely four, has just discovered a stretch of dune and water, an earthly version of paradise.

Thus begins the story of Benoît Bartherotte, the good wild man of Cap Ferret, on seeing Cap Ferret for the first time. Actually, it all began on the other side of the bay, in Arcachon, where for many years his family spent their vacations. It seemed that nothing could disrupt

12

*Above and right : The big
cabin, consists of a living
room and two bedrooms.
Collections of handicrafts,
handsome eighteenth
century rustic furniture.
Below : Under the roof
sits an old pump.*

the flow of those peaceful summers until, in the 1920's, the city began
to change, becoming more urbanized, and too much so for Benoît's
grandmother's tastes.

As a result, the family moved a few kilometers away to the less
civilized reaches of Mouleau, where they settled into two enormous
wooden cabins. This was the last stop before Pila, where they began
to sail across the bay to Cap Ferret.

Cap Ferret is a sand spit, almost an island, nearly deserted, tufted
with dune grass, that lies between the Gironde estuary and the bay of
Arcachon. For a long time there was no road, and the sea was its sole
means of access. « In the 1950's, the Point was our territory, » Benoît
Bartherotte recounts. « Along with a few other families, we had it all

16

to ourselves. Reaching it by land required perseverence, as the only road was always choked with sand. Covering the last hundred yards meant hacking a path through enormous broom bushes, and that could take an hour or two. Finally, we would make it to the beach, collapse onto the sand, and drink in the ocean with our eyes. We could never get enough of it.

« Our way of life was frankly minimalist, » Benoît Bartherotte remembers. « We rented cabins from the Teste fishermen, some so small you could hardly turn around in them. I called one the sleeping car! It was a dream of discomfort.

« We hauled water from a pump on the riverbank, and washed with big, sudsy sponges, sitting in old tubs overlooking the ocean.

« It was a time when summer vacations truly deserved their name: we deliberately cut ourselves off from the world for three whole months. » Back then, the young Benoît lived in the water or went sailing. His nautical exploits began in a dinghy.

« I got the idea of rigging a sort of mast—a stake from an oyster bed—and then improvising a sail. Finally I ventured forth on my first trip across the bay. I was perhaps six years old, and when I actually reached the other side, my heart was racing. It raced even faster when I realized I wouldn't be able to sail back against the wind. I had to row for nearly three miles—there was no other solution.

« The family greeted me rather coolly, but nothing could dim my joy. Along with my brothers and sisters, I was having too good a time. We knew every patch of dune by heart, and the wind sighing in the pine trees sang us to sleep at night. We were happy. »

So happy that Benoît would never forget the paradise of his childhood. For a long time, he dreamed about the tip of the point

Top left : An avid handyman, Adrien has slept with his toolbox since he was two.
Above : The children started riding Hasflinguer ponies when they were very little.
Above left : Against a background of palm trees, an outdoor work space, ideal for cleaning fish.

Houses in nature

where there is nothing but ocean as far as the eye can see, and the endlessly rolling dunes. Today, he lives there with his wife Zaza and their seven children in a little village of cabins—wooden ones, of course.

« We build them according to very strict specifications. They are made of pine from Landes, undressed timber; only the fireplaces are brick. They have to be low to the ground so the wind can't get a purchase on them, and also be easy to take apart since the dune and the sea are always shifting. Basically, these cabins are the realization of a dream I am recreating for my children, a tribe of children who learn independence fast, with the ease of those who have lived close to animals and nature since they were born.

« Water is their element, and animals are their friends. They've been raised with horses. Often, when I'm walking on the beach, I'll see a herd of young centaurs go galloping by in a whirlwind of sand; at other times, it will be the silhouette of a naked child asleep on his horse.

« We live in total harmony with nature, and, although we seek a certain solitude, we are not antisocial. We often set up huge tables of food in front of the big cabin and invite friends, family, carpenters, neighbors, all very casually. These meals are completely informal. People come and go, leaving the table as they wish. When Zaza no longer feels like seeing anyone, she retreats to her cabin. She is free, like everyone else here. »

Left and above : One of the bedrooms and the living room in the « blue house » : model boats, fine furniture. Above : The children display their art-work on a board wall in their parents' bedroom.

21

Left and above :

Lobster pot, boat ropes,

garden chairs,

fishing poles, propeller,

children in the sun :

the spirit of vacation.

23

AN ISLAND LOST AND FOUND

Certain old American families have been spending their summers on the Maine coast and its offshore islands since the turn of the century.

*M*aine is a region of stark and magnificent beauty, made to order for sports fanatics, sailing buffs, « polar bear club » swimmers, and for lovers of nature in its wildest state.

« This house has meant so much to us over the years, » muses Peter, seated on the wooden porch steps out of the wind. Between the pine trees, one glimpses the sea, and in the middle distance, a row of little islands, pristine and seemingly untouched by civilization. « My wife's great-grandfather discovered our island on a hiking trip. He bought it thinking it would be a perfect place for a golf course, which he constructed. Today, there's hardly anything left of it, but what does remain is this shingled

Wood-paneled walls,
family heirlooms,
accumulations of books
and kerosene lamps.
Nothing much has
changed since the house
was built in 1896.
<u>*Right :*</u> *The indispensable*
discussion of the day's
weather.

'cottage' he built in 1896 in a big clearing overlooking the sea. It's fairly sizable —twenty rooms—but families were larger in those days.

Thanks to him, the island and the house are essential parts of our lives today.

« Oddly enough, my family was involved with it, too. I remember my mother telling me how, as a young schoolteacher in Boston, she would take the overnight steamer to spend weekends here with Erica's grandmother, who taught at the same school. That was in 1932. I was five when she brought me to the island for the first time. When I was ten, I wrote in the guest book: 'Most important place I've ever been.' I think that still says it all. »

Now the cottage belongs to Peter. Alex, his son by a previous

marriage, has been coming here with him since early childhood and knows the place by heart. « Nothing has been changed since we moved in, » Peter says. « We like it the way it is. We haven't rearranged the furniture, or thrown anything away. It's all been carefully preserved, which means a lot to us. The plumbing was installed in 1904. I haven't even put in electricity—we still use the old kerosene lamps. »

Every year, in the spring, Peter, Erica and Alex open the house following a fixed schedule. « We dump the luggage on the front porch and then go around and unlock the back door, » he says. « Then we walk through the house opening all the windows and taking down the shutters. It never smells musty inside; it always smells like summer. »

Left : Nineteenth century chair, bureau, and period wallpaper add to the luminous atmosphere of the blue room.
Above : Details of a house where even the bears are on vacation.

Soon they slip back into the familiar traditions of their island lives, going to bed and getting up much earlier to take advantage of the daylight.

« Every morning, after breakfast, we meet for a sort of conference about the weather. After living here so long, and learning from the old salts who shared their knowledge with us, we never bother with the forecast on the radio anymore. Like everyone who lives on the ocean, we pay attention to subtle changes, shifts in the wind, and cloud formations. Our safety out on the water depends on knowing how to read these signs. »

Both father and son are excellent sailors. « When Alex was just a tiny tot, he was more at home on a boat than on land, » Peter explains. « At six, he rowed his little dinghy around like crazy, but we never worried when he headed offshore. The local fishermen, who are all our friends, kept an eye on him.

« We set great store on keeping our boats in top condition. They all have wooden hulls, and require constant scraping and painting.

« After a long day out on the water, right before dinner, we all troop in a procession down to the beach or over to the old golf course to look at the sunset. Views from a house shouldn't come too easy or it gets boring. Going to see the view makes it more important.

« I like to think that our great-grandparents and grandparents and parents did these same things before us.

« I find it deeply satisfying to feel the links that bind us to the past, and the comfort of knowing that life keeps repeating itself. »

Above : A loaf of olive bread ready for the oven.
Right : A big wood stove in its brick alcove.
Following double page : An expanse of sea visible through a clearing in the connifers. On the veranda, table and Chippendale chairs await the guests.

30

ARTISTS ON THE BEACH

Above : The artist Chuck Arnoldi and his son carve pumpkins for Halloween.
Right : At the edge of a steep cliff overlooking the Pacific, the house looks like an enormous rectangle with huge sliding doors.

Chuck Arnoldi is both an acclaimed artist and an architect. During the year, he lives with his wife, Katie, a competition body-builder, and their two children in Venice, California, an artist's community south of Los Angeles on the Pacific coast. There he has converted an immense warehouse into a studio and principle residence, and their lives are immersed in the worlds of art, design and fitness.

During the 1980's, however, the couple began to want to escape their career pressures and retreat to a second home for weekends and

34

Double preceding page :
On the garden side, the severe architecture of the house is beautifully integrated into the landscape.
Opposite : A restrained arrangement around a polished cement fireplace. The red leather chairs and couch provide a stark contrast to the black lava floor tiles. In front of the doors, three Oceanian totems stand guard.

vacations. Finally they found the ideal piece of land farther up the coast in Malibu, on top of a cliff that plunges to the beach below.

Comfortable with living in big rectangles, and as yet without children, they decided to build the shell of their new home first; a box that could subsequently be added. They would think about the interior design later. Now completed, the house is oriented toward the Pacific to the West and to the East opens onto a palm-fringed patio where the sky is reflected in the long narrow mirror of a lap pool.

The finished house reveals Arnoldi's mastery of volume, line and light. The hard edges of its angles soften as one experiences the space, while the simplicity of decor allows the mind to feel at peace.

Here the inside and the outside merge when the large
sliding doors are opened, giving the house an insubstantial,
airy feeling.

Furniture has been kept to a minimum without, however,
sacrificing a sense of comfort. It insinuates itself discretely in a
succession of fluid shapes organized around a monumental two-story
room. At intervals, wall panels accommodate Chuck Arnoldi's works,
and those of his artist friends.

One of California's principle charms is the fact that summer seems
to have settled here almost permanently, and the Arnoldis live in the
great outdoors; their two children spending three-quarters of the day
in the water bodysurfing with Chuck and running on the beach with

*Left : An austere
bathroom in which the
noon sun plays on the
gray plaster walls. Above :
In the bedroom, a glass
panel pivots opening onto
the living room.*

41

Katie. « I sometimes think they're going to grow fins. » Chuck laughs.
« The only thing that matters to us in Malibu is living at our own
pace and not worrying about anything, » he continues. « For the time
being, the children sleep on tatami mats in the closets off our
bedroom. They're still little, and have all the space in the world to
run around in during the day. I know that eventually my studio will
have to be turned into their bedroom, and I'll lose my bailiwick. But
that doesn't upset me. The important thing is knowing how to enjoy
the present moment. »

Left : Ryland plays on a
rug designed by his father.
Opposite and above : A
family scene : Katie in
deep conversation with her
son. Charles Eames
chairs.
Following double page :
A wooden staircase
gives access to
the beach.

Houses in nature

THREE GENERATIONS DOWN EAST

Above : The veranda
framed by a shingled
portico is a favorite
place for lunch.
Right : A wooded
landscape, a wild coastline
and a splendidly
isolated house.

A short boat ride off the coast of Maine, or « Down East, »
lies a small rocky island where deer stand fearlessly in the clearings
and tame squirrels scramble through the pine trees. Nothing has
changed for a long time. The few families who summer here lead
simple lives close to nature.

The island is cut off from the world, its one link with the
mainland being mailboat and a launch that comes only if called by
telephone. After landing, everyone carries his or her own bags along
the shore path and up through a dense forest, the heavier loads going

46

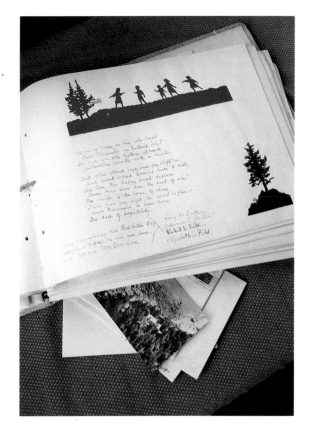

by wheelbarrow since no vehicles are allowed.

Barbara Rosenthal, a musician from New York, has spent the past 37 summers in one of the shingled houses scattered along the top of the bluff overlooking the sparkling blue Maine water. She first came to the island with her composer husband, and fell in love with the house, which, quite by coincidence, contained a pair of Steinway concert grand pianos, along with large, comfortable furnishings and oriental rugs. Now a grandmother, Mrs. Rosenthal summers there with her friends and family.

Life on the island takes on its own rhythm—reading in the sunroom in the morning, kyacking or sailing in the afternoon, and cooking in the large country kitchen at the end of the day.

Far left : On the mantle in the living room, a colony of sea urchins. Right : The family dog, a constant companion. Above : Navigational books, writing paper with nautical scenes and a ship's log : life on the island is completely focused on the sea.

49

*Sailboats, teddy bears,
rag doll form
the backdrop for a perfect
place to read. Following
double page : Early in the
morning, the children can
be seen climbing on the
rocks.*

As Mrs. Rosenthal looks back on her many Maine seasons, it is memories of her children's summers here that bring her the most pleasure. « I was always happy that they grew up partly on the island with no cars, no stores, no TV, and no toys, » she says. « They were only allowed to bring one toy each year, so they learned to 'play' with what the island itself offered. The tidal pools were unending sources of limpets and mussels for the shell pictures they made, and grocery boxes became animal and doll houses. I think this taught them self-reliance, and encouraged imagination. The island patriarch came every week to read the Bible to them, and then we'd watch the sunset from the rocks below the house. The two magical yearly events for our family were always Christmas and going to Maine. »

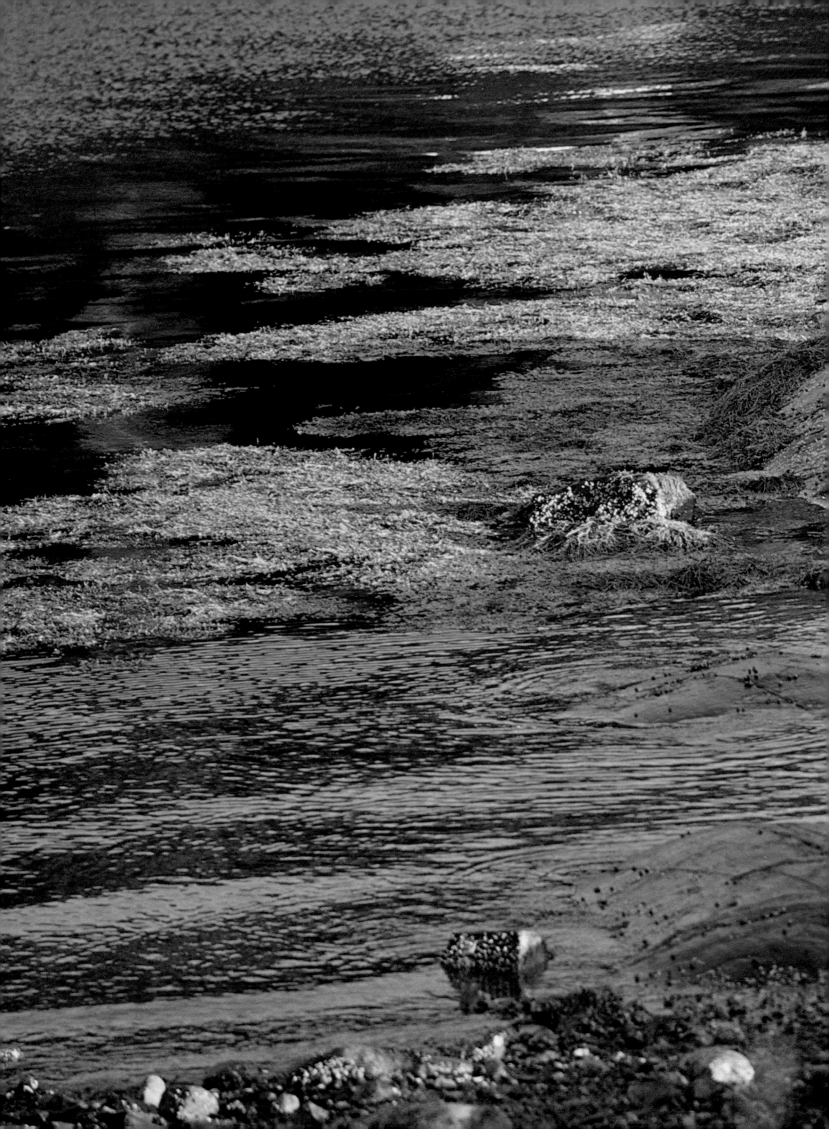

FAMILY FISHING

Chappaquiddick is a tiny island off Martha's Vineyard in Massachusetts, a mixture of beach and scrub pine woods to which Lindsay and Blake Allison return each summer with their children, Morgan and Sam. For generations the island has been the traditional rallying point for their relatives: Lindsay's mother and aunt each own a house near Whitherwind. During the summer, the members of this close-knit family wander back and forth between the three houses as if each were home.

Whitherwind lies at the end of a private road that winds between a

54

succession of flower and herb gardens, and immense sweeps of lawn.
Located on more than 500 feet of private beach, one side faces
Katama Bay and the port of Edgartown, and the other faces a
backdrop of woods and clearings, fields and ponds, crisscrossed by
walking trails.

Whitherwind, the oldest of the shingled houses, boasts a screened
porch and two covered verandas. In the large eat-in kitchen, an old
sideboard contains a seemingly inexhaustible store of homemade jams
and preserves. A fleet of little sailboats hanging from a beam, a bunch

*Left : Whitherwind is a
large family house.
Above : The whole family
loves fishing.
Below : After the beach,
the boys take turns at the
outdoor shower.*

Houses in nature

Above : Pale colors in the living room and navigational charts on the walls. Right : On the couch, slipcovered in finely striped cotton, the geometric stars of a patchwork quilt.

of flowers picked on a walk, a few photos and shelves of books bespeak the casual tone.

Off the kitchen, the living room, full of comfortable sofas, armchairs, tables and reading lamps, welcomes those who like to spin out the evening around the wood stove, after the family meal. Here, the navigational charts on the wall recall the sea outside.

The long happy days blend together, with fishing off the family boat, clamming, and strolling along the beach looking for shells to add to the collection gathered over past vacations. Lindsay is a great fisherwoman, and often goes surf casting on the south shore of the island, alone or with her son and daughter. Although crews of serious local fishermen are usually churning up and down the beach in jeeps

One thinks of a library or
a dining room when one
enters this large, convivial
kitchen where a fleet of
little sailboats hanging
from the ceiling adds a
touch of humor. *Above :*
The message corner, with
the often referred to tide
table.

Above : A bathroom where nothing has changed since the house was built. Top : The white-painted ceiling in the attic bedroom. Right : A room designed around a patchwork quilt ; all the furniture has been painted red.

looking for the diving gulls that mean fish are feeding below, she enjoys the general frenzy. Sometimes, when she's lucky, she has the whole beach to herself, and then the slow, rhythmical casting and reeling in of her lure is « meditative and relaxing, » she says.

When the fishermen return, everyone gathers on the porch with a glass of iced tea, perhaps joined by friends and the editor of the local newspaper, to swap fish stories and local gossip. At night, they feast on the ultrafresh striped bass or bluefish from their catch, relishing the joy of being together as a family.

Later, settled on a windowseat in the living room's big bay window, Sam and his dog will probably fall asleep, lulled by the peaceful whisper of the waves.

A COTTAGE ON A CLIFF

Above : On the flat moors
the fishermen's cottages are
covered with thatch.
Right : On the stone
wall that surrounds
the garden ; a few
moments of peace.

he Isle of Wight: an uncompromising landscape you learn to love young, which stays with you all your life.

« We've been coming to the Isle forever, » says Kate. « My family hails from here, and that creates ties. Before, when we were living on the estate, my grandmother had a passion for this fisherman's cottage. It was, and still is, miniscule—that's part of its charm. When I'm in the living room with its thick walls and narrow windows, I feel like a rabbit in its burrow, cozy and safe from harm.

« On stormy days, I have the impression of being in the bow of a

sturdy little ship, quite intrepid, very stalwart. It's also in this room that we set up the « big » pine tree at Christmas; the « little » one is in the other room.

« We come here often in winter, a privileged time of year when we feel entirely cut off from the world. The days are very short. We live holed up indoors talking, playing Monopoly, and simply enjoying the warmth of the fire.

« In summer, it's a whole other story. We're outdoors all day long living the kind of simple life that give you a huge appetite. That's probably why, when we were children, picnics were often on the agenda. I adored our cookouts on the beach: they were quite acrobatic expeditions, actually, because we had to scramble down the

Top left : The sun room, adjoining the house and facing the garden, catches every ray of sunshine. Flowered chintz curtains and a linen bed throw. Bottom : A child's bedroom with a captain's bed. Above : In the living room, a still life with poppies.

Houses in nature

face of the cliff lugging our baskets of food to get there. My father would build an enormous bonfire with driftwood it was our mission to collect, and we'd roast sausages threaded onto long skewers, our cheeks burning and our eyes smarting from the smoke.

« On the subject of picnics, there were the simpler ones we carried along with us on our boat. Since the boat wasn't very big, and it never occurred to us not to take our three dogs, and the two-legged crew already numbered four children plus my father, Mama, who wasn't very seagoing, would plead overcrowdedness and leave us to our fate.

« Mama likes the sea but prefers the roses she grows behind the house in the part of the garden that's sheltered from the wind.

« Roses are the joy of my youngest son, aged five, whose specialty is a perfume based on rose petals, mint leaves and exotic spices. »

Above : On the kitchen shelves, papered, like the walls, in a small floral print, the breakfast dishes.
Right : White wainscoting, enameled metal trays, checked cotton tablecloth, furniture painted blue : the kitchen where the boys bake cookies on rainy days.
Following double page : As far as the eye can see, a wall of cliffs battered by the waves.

66

WIND AND WAVES

Above : White on white accented by ceiling moldings, window frames, a pine floor and the pale linen covers on the caned and carved nineteenth century Anglo-Indian furniture.

Right : The steps lead down to the dune grass.

Double following page : Kilkare, where tradition is respected.

hy some houses are like no other house in the world, but are utterly unique, is, of course, a mystery. Perhaps, in the case of Kilkare, it's the way this gray-shingled house, surmounting the crest of a dune, seems to challenge the horizon. At its feet lies the immense, empty beach crowned with rugosa rose and beach plum, and precariously guarded from erosion by rickety snow fences held together with rusty wires. Beyond, the Atlantic Ocean stretches all the way to Portugal.

On this surf-pounded coast of eastern Long Island, in the

70

now-trendy Hamptons, it seemed that nothing could disturb the solitude of this lonely sentinel, which stood empty for a long time. But now it is animated by the joyous energy of the Kennedy family, who finally bought the historic house a few years ago.

One can almost glimpse the diaphanous shadows of the bygone ladies of the turn-of-the-century when Kilkare was constructed by a shipbuilding dynasty. Corseted, wasp-waisted, their long skirts flirtily raised to reveal a hint of ankle, they might be taking tea on the big second-floor veranda. Or playing croquet on the lawn, wide-brimmed bonnets tied with silk ribbons protecting their pale skin from the sun.

In those days, Kilkare employed a staff of eleven servants, the only task of one being to tend the fires in the many fireplaces, keeping the

Left : The dining room with its white-painted brick fireplace. Above : A collection of shells from the beach with names written on them. The shells are used as place cards for the big nineteenth century table.

75

damp sea air from this sailors' landmark. It is said that two ghosts still haunt the place, perhaps a lady gazing out to sea and houseboy keeping a watchful eye on the glowing embers.

The house came to Michael and Eleanor Kennedy's attention one February in a magazine ad that said « A Gift from the Sea. » Although the place was dreadfully run-down and had suffered wind and water damage during its vacancy, « nothing matters when you fall in love, » as Mrs. Kennedy put it. « You don't think of practical things. »

Today, thanks to scrupulous restoration, Kilkare's beautiful architecture has been brought back to life, providing sanctuary from the New York whirl. « It has a monastic feeling that is truly liberating, » Mrs. Kennedy explains. « It is a place where we can think,

and indulge ourselves in nature. » It is also a warm family house, and hospitable to their many friends.

On Monday nights between Memorial Day and Labor Day, there are beach parties organized by the Georgica Association, a local property-owners group. A gigantic bonfire is lit, and everyone barbecues meats and vegetables they have marinated all day. The children roast marshmallows for dessert on willow branches it is Michael Kennedy's responsibility to provide.

The Kennedys also come here year round, never tiring of the changing seasons. Each fall, they wait for the arrival of the Canada geese who now winter in the area. In late October, Michael takes over the kitchen to hollow out pumpkins and carve them

A succession of family pictures link the past and the present. On the upright piano, a score is waiting for music lesson's time.

77

In a pine-paneled bedroom, a nineteenth century four-poster bed covered with an old fashioned spread. The furniture and lamps, all original pieces, have been restored by the Kennedys. In the window, an antique baptismal dress.

into jack-o'-lanterns for Halloween night.

In winter, there is ice skating on the pond in the village of East Hampton, a Currier and Ives setting of old-fashioned charm. On Christmas Eve, the whole family bundles up and drives to midnight Mass past the rows of lighted trees that line Main Street.

In spring, when nature comes alive again, they pay discreet visits to the many swans who raise their young on small ponds in the vicinity. And all year long, beside the magnificent ocean, there is time to read, talk, and cook; time, as Mrs. Kennedy puts it, for the family to « nest » like the swans.

Above : Paneled bathrooms with cast iron tubs on claw feet and porcelain sinks. Right : A marvelous natural wicker bed draped with a nineteenth century American cream silk shawl. Following double page : Out on the beach.

80

A MEDITERRANEAN SUMMER

Built on a cliff overlooking the sea, the house was inspired by the little temples in Kyoto.
Right : Immense glass panels frame the vegetation, creating a link between the exterior and the interior. An 1880 bamboo bird cage evokes a Chinese pagoda.
Following double page : The house is surrounded by wide decks.

Certain houses are like a child's fantasy...

« I always dreamed of a house in the trees », Nathalie muses aloud, « one that would be large enough for my whole family. A real summer house—cool, with no rugs or curtains, and completely open to the outdoors. A house that would be sort of like a boat with gangways, decks and bridges. »

One day, her dream came true. On a hilltop beside the Mediterranean, the Belgian landscape painter Michel Delvosalle designed a house on pilings for Nathalie, a house in the treetops

84

overlooking the sea, subtly integrated into the precipitous countryside
where cicadas drone in the steady heat. A path carpeted with pine
needles winds down the cliff to the flat rocks along the shore where
the family goes to swim.

When the sun gets too hot, a column of tanned backs, straw hats
at odd angles, and shoulders with towels thrown over them, can be
seen straggling up the hill to the restful shade of the living room.
Sandals and espadrilles are dropped at the doorstep, and everyone
walks barefoot across the cool floor for a glass of the chilled rosé
awaiting them in the fridge. It's time for lunch and then a siesta.

Local foods are set out on the counter in front of the kitchen:
black olives, crisp cucumbers, cheese, sweet melon, and flat bread

Left : All the bedrooms
face the sea.
Above : The whole house
is built of Oregon pine.
In the spacious living
room, the couch and
chairs are covered with a
Guatemalan print. Beside
the kitchen, a sculptured
staircase leads to a balcony
where windsurfers are
stored. _Below :_ A white
bathroom in the great
outdoors.

typical of the Midi. When it's this hot, no one's ever very hungry, but they perch on the bar stools and fix themselves a light snack. After lunch, not even the very strong coffee can dispel the delicious lethargy that overcomes the household.

In a while, perhaps the children will go back down to the water with their windsurfers. Others will do the shopping in the nearby village: eggplant, zucchini, green and red peppers, tomatoes and plenty of garlic for the evening's ratatouille. Then they'll stop for a pastis at the cafe and watch the pétanque players in the square. Back home, the air will smell of pine and myrtle, and the heat will persist; even the parakeets will tuck their heads under their wings.

The guests drift off, some disappearing into their rooms. Those who prefer to stay outdoors relax in lounge chairs on the deck and settle down with old novels. On the sea below, armadas of boats cruise the channels, unfurling foamy wakes behind them.

Eyes half-closed, the readers follow their comings and goings. Nothing moves except for a slight breeze in the garden. The cicadas grow shriller. Time stands still. Later, the more energetic of the group will go down for one last swim in a sea so transparent the bottom seems to rise up to meet the surface.

The afternoon ends, and the children wash and put on clean shorts and T-shirts. The grown-ups change out of their beach skirts and bathing suits. Everyone meets on the terrace to await the pink flush that spreads from the horizon and envelops the hill as the sun sinks slowly into the sea. The table is set. The ratatouille is cooling. Soon, the cicadas will fall silent. Then dinner will be served by the trembling light of hurricane lamps as the stars prick through the blue velvet of the Mediterranean night sky...

Above : Tall hieratic silhouettes stand guard along the shore.
Right : On the wooden deck, facing the Mediterranean, the slate table which seems to be suspended from the trees.

THE CALIFORNIA LIFE

Above : The house, built of red cedar bleached gray, is all one level. At the bottom of the steps, facing the sea, the swimming pool is flush with the deck. Right : Every room has its own large balcony. Following double page : Sun blinds soften the austere structure of the house.

*B*uilding a dream house for your family in your mind's eye is a delightful exercise—especially if the dream becomes reality some day. « We wanted to spend our summers in a house that was like a balcony overlooking the sea, » the young woman explained. « No question of restoring an old building. We wanted to create a house made to order for our vacations. »

The place? That was more or less a foregone conclusion since her husband had scuba-dived for twenty years off the Lavezzi Islands in the southernmost part of Corsica, a harsh, primitive region whose

rugged beauty is softened there by the extraordinary transparency of the Mediterranean. It is a place they already knew well and loved.

They bought a piece of wild, brushy land right on the water, a few kilometers outside Bonifacio. The architect Boguslaw Brzeckowski, in close collaboration with the couple, designed a house of gray-bleached cedar, all on one level except for a lookout room on a promontory with a wraparound view of the sea, and the surrounding islands and mountains. Victor, Arthur and David, the couple's three sons, would have their own little house, connected to the big one by a boardwalk.

The main building consists of a vast living room, the parents' quarters and the guest rooms. Outside, a swimming pool with a panoramic view adjoins a flight of steps that leads to a succession of

Far left : In the immense living room, facing the sea, the dining area. Left, right : In the main room, furnished very simply in teak, pale blue Venetian blinds filter the light. Below : On a wall of shelves, the shell collection.

97

large decks, also made of wood, that surround the entire house.

The indoors and the outdoors seem to merge thanks to the unity of colors and materials used throughout. Inside, furniture and objects have been kept to a minimum, and plain white linen curtains filter the intense light coming through the huge sliding glass doors opening onto the sea. The floor is made of wide boards painted with gray deck enamel, amazingly cool under bare feet, that give an impression of space, but also of freedom and serenity, making the world seem very far away.

It took a year before the family finally settled in and began to form the habits and patterns that gradually evolved into its rites of summer. The morning starts with breakfast on the deck, the Mediterranean as

backdrop, where plans for the day, preferably of a sporting nature, are made. Then everyone disperses. Some go running, others play tennis, while others simply find a place to relax. The boys generally go down to the beach on the path that winds around the hillside, unless they suddenly decide to take their motorboat across the strait to Sardinia and lunch on pasta and seafood at a waterfront restaurant. On the way back, they might stop for a swim and, home by late afternoon, still have time for a few sets of tennis before dark.

In the evening, the boys eat at a table covered with blue oilcloth, too tired even to notice the astonishingly beautiful sunset. But tomorrow a new day will dawn, and with it another chance to settle into their newly established rites of summer.

Left : One of the guest rooms, its angled walls covered by wide wooden boards. Above : A seating area around the fireplace. Large painted wood birds from Australia.

99

Opposite : Simple and
practical, a children's
bedroom with bunk beds
designed by the owners.
Above : The white-tiled
bathroom ; its raised tub
looks out on the view.

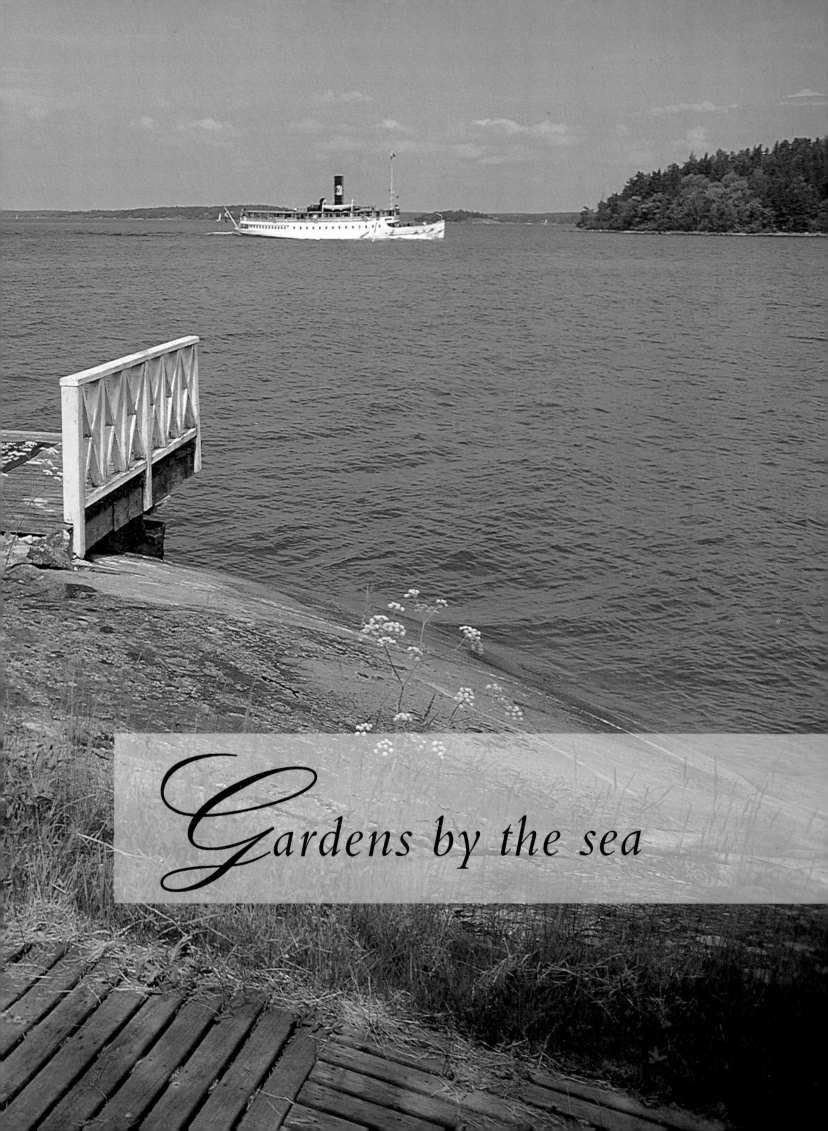

Gardens by the sea

Not all seaside houses have their feet in the sand and their heads in the blazing sun. Some are nestled into farming country, or stand in a landscape of moors or forests. And then there is England, where almost every acre resembles a Constable painting with gently rolling fields, little woods, and coves shaded by century-old trees. Here gardens, bordered by low stone walls, stop at the water's edge: the bucolic and the sea merged in perfect harmony.

Elsewhere, as in the land around Caux, one sees shorelines with a harsher aspect; steep faces of white cliffs rising against the sky. In Sweden, in the Stockholm archipelago where the view sweeps across the water to Finland, the landscape is brushy, wooded, with houses like children's drawings, and hills with rocky flanks that plunge into the sea. On the coast of Maine, one finds wilderness still haunted by the memory of proud Indian tribes. Along these varied coastlines, the houses seem to play hide-and-seek with the ocean. Concealed in the undergrowth, standing at the border of an English park, or perched on the edge of a wood, they tend to be large dwellings, spacious and comfortable. Living in them over the years, one discovers that they have a heart; to hear its beat, one must know how to listen.

Gardens by the sea

GIVERNY·BY·THE·SEA

*S*ituated in an English park on the crest of a chalky cliff, the house, a few minutes from Varengeville, is signed Luytens, a rarity in France where the brilliant British architect only designed two residences, both for the Baron Mallet. Guillaume Mallet was a pure product of the nineteenth century, a banker by profession and, by temperament, an art lover and patron of the arts.

If the baron chose to locate his summer quarters in the Caux region, it was not by chance but was a question of returning to his origins, for his ancestors possessed huge holdings in the area, where one of them had fought at William the Conqueror's side.

He refused to succumb—good Protestant that he was—to the allure the resort of Dieppe had for his contemporaries, preferring, to its frivolity and worldly bustle, the peaceful rhythms of Varengeville, a little village already appreciated by painters, nestled among the trees two steps from the sea.

In 1878, he had charged his architect with the task of building him a town house. Evidently gratified by this experience, he placed an order in 1909 for a summer residence for his three children, the one that concerns us here. Luytens opted for the « butterfly design, » highly esteemed in the Edwardian era. The house, in the shape of a Y, consists of three wings, slightly bowed, which act as

107

windbreaks while at the same time directing the maximum amount of
sunlight into the interior: an original concept, and perfectly suited to
the region's capricious climate. One notices the influence of the Arts
and Crafts Movement, but the roof, with its curved pitch, remains
faithful to local tradition.

In front of the lavender-bordered terrace, a vast lawn framed by
great trees provides a view to the edge of the cliff where, through an
optical illusion, the water seems to rise to meet the land: the joys of
the country and those of the sea commingled.

Here the atmosphere was less formal than in the town house.
Following the baron's example, family and friends savored the bracing
air without, however, negelecting needs of the spirit. The day began

with a reading aloud, often a passage from Shakespeare. Eschewing bourgeois constraints, the family received bohemians, artists and even theosophists, and the young Krishnamuti and his brother were doted upon.

« No one who has stayed here has ever forgotten it, » explains the present owner. « That is partly due to the character of the place, but also to the exceptional personalities of the people who have lived within these walls. When I fell in love with the house, I longed to spend as much time here as possible.

« This is a seafaring community where you don't go out in a boat simply for pleasure; you go to fish. And you have to watch out for the rather changeable weather, the squalls that come up suddenly. There's a strong current out there, not much depth, and no shelter. The port of Dieppe, like Saint-Valery-en-Caux, is very difficult to enter. A treacherous surf can build up without warning, as the many wrecks stranded on the shore attest. The sea around here is for professionals only. There are a few hardy souls who swim in the glacial water, but you have to be knowledgeable about the tides to risk it. You'll often see old natives on the road in their bathrobes, going home after a dip.

« During the holidays, at low tide, the family goes looking for mussels and various kinds of crabs, but fishing for prawns is by far the most challenging. You have to wear waders that come up to your waist to protect yourself from the cold. Prawns live among the rocks, and everyone has his own tricks for taking them. It's exhausting work because the nets are extremely heavy, and their handles very long and hard to control. Sometimes you lose your balance and fall, and your waders fill with water—then moving at all is a challenge. Sometimes

you comb the area for hours, with less than brilliant results. Of course, that's when your appetite is at its most ferocious.

« From my bedroom, I can hear the foghorn on the Ailly lighthouse in the distance, piercing the night. When I'm half awake, I love listening to the bell buoys clanging out in the open sea. Then one last thought crosses my mind—the wind is going to change—and I fall sleep.

« In this house, which is so much a part of the land, the link with the sea is its smell: the smell of the tides, and of seaweed, which rises over the cliff at the end of the garden. In these parts, we have two kinds of weather; sea weather, which is damp and cool, and land weather which is always hot and dry.

Left : A book-lined office with muted walls. Above : A piano lesson. The living room occupies an entire wing of the house which was designed by Luytens in the shape of a Y.

111

Above left : The cliffs of Varengeville, sources of inspiration for Monet and Renoir.
Above right :
Under a painting by Philippe Dumas, a bouquet from the garden.
Right : A little girl reading seated in a large colonial chair of woven rattan.

« When we're not fishing, or in the garden, or playing tennis, we hunt. Or mainly I do. This activity is also linked to the sea, since curlews, plovers and herons live to the rhythm of the winds and tides. We hunt on an incoming tide, when the wind is from the northeast.

« We start off either at dawn or at dusk, and walk a long time. Sometimes we hide in blinds. With the first cold snaps of November, we'll be gone for the whole day. Then I often spend the night in a hut out in the marsh with my Labrador retriever, and at dawn we move out and lie in wait for the birds to fly over.

« It's a magical, moment, when you feel in harmony with nature. This kind of hunting is only for people who love birds. I never shoot anything my family and I won't eat later; that's a house rule. »

112

AUTUMN SONATA

*S*olgArd can be recognized from a distance by the twin outbuildings—one a boathouse, the other a sauna and bath house— standing at the water's edge. It is impossible, however, to see the big house hidden discreetly in the vegetation; you have to get closer to the beach. Then, on a hill, an elegant manor emerges from the trees, a pure product of the island in its grand old days, just after the turn of the century.

Built in 1912 by the celebrated architect Ivar Tengborm, SolgArd is a masterpiece of harmony and balance, no doubt because Tengborm

saw to everything himself, down to the last detail.

This created a certain tension between the architect and the father of the present owner, who was also the foreman of the building crew. The latter, for example, wanted the walls of the entrance hall to be painted yellow, a color that evoked in his mind the name of the house, in English, « House of the Sun. » Tengborm finally gave in to his wish, however, and the highly controversial yellow proved to be a great success.

SolgArd, which faces northwest, overlooks the sea. Thanks to its

Left : The house, built at the turn of the century by Ivar Tengborm, overlooks the sea. _Above :_ Relaxing moments « en famille » on the veranda. Two buildings on the shore welcome visiting boats.

115

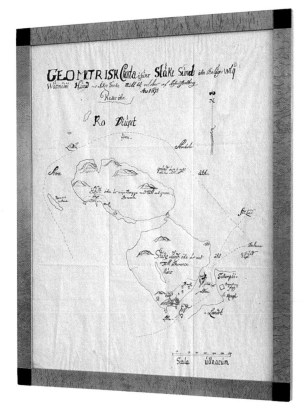

enormous windows, it seems to be flooded with light all day and, during the summer, is bathed in an opalescent half-light all night. In the dining room, huge glass doors frame an incredible panorama: the sea as far as the eye can see.

At SolgArd, certain well-established traditions are still observed. Today, as in the past, on occasions of celebration—birthdays or when friends are expected—the gravel courtyard is carefully raked, and the flag is flown.

Then a buffet made entirely of hors d'oeuvres a smorgasbord, is served on the veranda which the guests sample before sitting down to dinner.

Per Wästberg, a writer who spent several summers here,

Left : On the dock, whose design echos the woodwork on the house, the Swedish flag is about to be raised. Above : The French doors with curiously shaped, rounded panes open onto the balcony. The map of the island, made by hand, dates from 1693.

remembers in one of his books *Sommaröarna* (*The Islands of Summer*) the wonderful moments savored at the end of the season: « In autumn, the island is wrapped in nostalgia, a nostalgia made all the more poignant by the ephemeral joys of the beautiful summer just past. The memory of water lapping under the dock and of the trembling reflection of the sun filtering through the cracks between its boards will remain in everyone's mind, even in the depths of winter. The memory also of the damp odor of the piles of dead leaves, the slightly salty smell that rises from the sea, and the aroma of wood warmed by the sun. »

Preceding double page : In the living room, furniture in the style of Karl Johan, the Swedish Biedemeier. On the desk, an eighteenth century porcelain soup tureen and a family portrait painted by J. A. G. Acke. Above left : The blue and red kitchen. Above: The lunch buffet.

In a guest room, a large map of the Stockholm archipelago covers the wall.

UNDER THE MIDNIGHT SUN

*A*ngled toward the meadow and the bay, Djurö Gästgiveri clings precariously to the edge of a wood. This former inn, once very run-down, is now the summer house of Björn and Monika Sahlström and their children and, thanks to them, has regained the elegant look it had in the eighteenth century.

The Sahlströms bravely undertook a veritable labor of restoration, bringing to light, for example, some lovely panelling that had been buried under successive layers of wallpaper. The only major addition is a new veranda which enlarges the space without altering its

The feast of Saint John's Day, enthusiastically celebrated by the whole family. In the background, the house and the sauna.

124

Preceding double pages :
The enormous lawn is the
center of all kinds of
games as well as the dance
around the Saint John
Maypole. Left : In the
wood-paneled living
room, the King Gustavus
chest of drawers dates from
the eighteenth century, as
does the mirror in the
entryway (Opposite).
Above : A portrait of
King Gustavus III.

Gardens by the sea

character. Inside, the King Gustavus style has been retained, with its tonalities of white and blue that echo the colors of the sea and sky.

Beside the sea, on a large rock, a cabin painted red houses the indispensable sauna as well as a guest room. Djurö Gästgiveri is open year-round, and the Sahlströms go there whenever they have an opportunity. Nothing deters them—not even winter when the countryside is buried in snow and the house plunged into the endless night of northern countries.

At these times, parents and children huddle together around the enamel wood stove, while fires burn brightly in all the bedrooms. It's cozy and warm indoors and, in the benign calm, everyone forgets the cold night outside.

Pinned to the wall, a seating plan and list of preparations for the celebration. Right : The guest room in the sauna house, built on a rock beside the sea.

130

The family waits patiently for spring and, when it finally comes, greets it with the joyous feast of Saint John, celebrating new growth and the return of light. There is a gathering of relatives and friends for which each person makes enthusiastic preparations. The grown-ups' tasks are written on a list thumbtacked to the wall: the women busy themselves in the kitchen while the men set up the Saint John Maypole, festooning it with garlands, and placing big bowls of flowers throughout the house. Weather permitting, the meal is served out doors on the lawn. Otherwise, the feasting takes place on the veranda, and in the adjoining dining room. Then there is accordion music and dancing around the Maypole, through the garden and down to the dock, far into the brightening night of the midnight sun.

On the veranda, a large King Gustavus couch. Following double page : The dining room chairs and the big enamel corner stove are of the King Gustavus period.

Gardens by the sea

131

A PASSION FOR BOATS

*Crowned by a bell tower
that serves as an
observatory during the
famous Cowes regattas,
the house is surrounded
by a garden designed
in the eighteenth century.*

*T*he history of Cardland Manor, at once beautiful, tragic and happy, is exemplary. It begins in the middle of the eighteenth century when a descendant of a noble and ancient Scotch line decided to settle on a family property in Hampshire overlooking The Solent, that arm of sea which separates the Isle of Wight from southern England. The site is of a rare beauty, ideal for building a house worthy of a man of quality. The project was entrusted to two renowned architects, Henry Holland and Capability Brown.

The stately residence, ornamented by an elegant portico supported

134

Left and above : A comfortable, elegant decor for the world of the lord of the manor, a naval historian with collections of nautical almanacs, portraits of famous admirals, and extraordinary ship models like the one of the H.M.S. Alarm, a frigate built in 1758. Opposite : A ship's log illustrated in pen and watercolor.

137

by Ionic columns, was completed in 1778. Five large bay windows opened onto the Solent, a busy sea lane crowded with ships. At a little distance, almost in the water, the architects conceived a sort of eighteenth century-style fisherman's cottage, never for a moment suspecting the important place this pretty building would later occupy in the family affections.

It was reached by a gravel drive, soothingly shaded by tall trees and propitious for walking. Facing the Isle of Wight, the cottage had a thatched roof and was graced by a veranda. It was small, however, and was used mainly for storing fishing poles and nets, and as a place to rest after boat rides. While no one actually lived there, peaceful hours were spent in this idyllic setting. In the summer, picnics and dinner

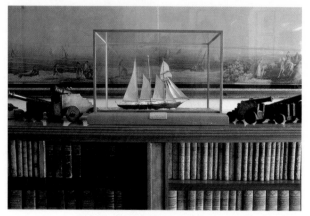

parties followed in close succession, and it was during one of these receptions that a tragedy occurred in 1785.

On that night, a shower of sparks flew from the kitchen and set the roof on fire. According to legend, the lord of the manor, exhibiting typical British « sang-froid » as well as an unerring taste in vintages, raced down to the cellar to remove his best bottles to a safe distance from the disaster. The fire brought under control, he served an impromptu supper to his guests—what a shining example of « savoir-vivre » !

The cottage was quickly rebuilt, enlarged, and wisely roofed, this time with slate.

During the First World War, after a century and a half of relative tranquility, a second fire again burned the cottage to the ground while it was rented out for the season. Twenty-one people were living in it at the time, including eight children, but, fortunately, no one was hurt.

The cottage lay in ruins until the beginning of the 1930's, when it rose again from the ashes. Its heir want so far in his esteem for it as to retrieve and clean every brick that had been blackened by the fire. The new walls, constructed in part of these old materials, are in a way the « memory » of the building that now occupies the cottage site.

Today, nothing has really changed at Cardland Manor. The days are peaceful, lived to the schedule of the local yacht races. The present owner, a great sailor and naval historian, has assembled an exceptional collection of ship models which are displayed alongside his numerous family souvenirs. His wife, for her part, has restored the gardens to their former splendor, helping her husband forge strong new links in the chain that will no doubt be carried forward by their young son, connecting the past with the future of this historic estate.

Left : Vivid yellow in the ground floor closet. On the nineteenth century chest of drawers, the model of a fishing boat. A nineteenth century telescope in a room like a ship's cabin. Following double page : Everything to delight a little boy is in this bright, lively and studious room where a mahogany bed is built into two bookcases.

Gardens by the sea

LIKE A SHIPWRECKED BARN

*A house the size of
an old-fashioned barn
with boats anchored
below.*

he sky is a tranquil blue broken only by little clusters of puffy clouds. Below, in a cove nestled in a patchwork of fields—their delicate acid green still a British secret—a fleet of small boats peacefully bobs at anchor. A blond boy crouching on a sunny bank draws circles in the water. A second boy swings idly on a long rope tied to the stout branch of an old tree, then jumps to the ground and joins his brother. What are they plotting? A fishing trip? A boat ride?

In the boat house next to the studio where their father carves shorebirds, at least a dozen more boats of all different kinds are ready

146

to set sail, while close to shore the gaff-rigged ketch *Vivette* tugs lazily at her mooring. When no distant port of call is on the vacation agenda, the whole family, including the dog, often takes the *Vivette* out for an evening picnic on the beach. They also frequently sail her up the coast and spend the day exploring its various bays and inlets.

A seaweed forest undulates on the bottom. On a piling a few yards offshore, a carved wooden sea gull perches, the emblem of Seagull House, home of Roderick and Gillie James, their three sons Daniel, Ben and Woody, and, of course, their dog Rocky. Situated slightly above the curve of the bay, just at the edge of a wood looking out on both the water and a charmingly informal garden, Seagull House resembles a huge shipwrecked boat washed up onshore, a boat with

Left : The shed serves as a storeroom for the whole family and a bedroom for Rocky. Above : A big gas stove and a cupboard filled with simple china. Flour and biscuits are stored in stoneware crocks in this kitchen off the living room.

149

*When it's dark outside,
Gillie James turns on all
the spotlights in the white
studio where she makes
her quilts.*

the majestic proportions of an old-fashioned barn.

There is nothing surprising about this. Roderick James, an architect by profession, is a sailing enthusiast who has many shipbuilders, not to mention sailors, in his family tree, dating back to 1850. One of his greatuncles was chief engineer on the first steam-driven coast guard cutter, which sank off Cornwall in 1900. A man with that much saltwater in his veins could never live very far from the sea.

The « barn » aspect of the house is linked to a long period the Rodericks spent in the country during which James had plenty of time to study a number of old barns.

Finding them at once spacious, solid and elegant, he resolved not

only to build one for himself beside the sea, but also to produce and market his modern designs throughout the world. Today, both of his ambitions have been realized.

Seagull House, which actually consists of three separate houses, was significantly changed by the addition of a huge glassed-in porch. The roof was also raised and the walls paneled in wood; but while the results were aesthetically pleasing, there still was not enough room. The size of the family and the diverse activities of each member called for more space.

Daniel and Woody are content to share a room. But Ben, who plays guitar, Gillie, who likes to hole up for the afternoon working on her patchwork quilts, and Roderick, with his passion for model ships,

Left and above : In the entryway and living room, the tinted plaster walls range from a deep rose to a sunny terra-cotta. In the living room, the rattan furniture is purposefully subdued in contrast to the bright colors and prints.

153

*Opposite and above :
Blond and pastel shades
in the guest room and
adjoining bath, paneled in
natural pine. An
unexpected and successful
mixture of styles : two
large nineteenth century
portraits in gilt frames
dominate a plain white
iron bed covered with one
of Gillie James's quilts.*

all needed a room of their own. A first barn is connected to the main house by a few steps and serves as Gillie's studio, while on an upper level Ben occupies a room in the treetops. A door in the studio leads to Roderick's barn, a cathedral-like space in which one feels at home despite the structure's imposing height.

To allow the sun to move freely through this blond oak universe, certain walls have been replaced by glass partitions, and the roof has been opened up with stained glass windows. Gillie, the colorist of the family, chose the panes of glass to match the pastel shades of the flowers growing in the garden.

At Christmas, this room is decorated by the children and their father: they cover the walls with branches of holly and mistletoe, and stand a gigantic fir tree in the middle, so tall it touches the ceiling, its piney scout filling the room.

But day to day, the room is completely functional. Isolated in its beautiful, luminous space, Roderick has the peace to work, think, and render plans while his wife sews next door, Ben practices his music, and Woody pursues his interests such as building a luxurious kennel for Rocky. As for Daniel, he's just a little dot on the horizon, skimming over the tops of the waves on his Windsurfer.

Everyone is occupied until it's time to gather before dinner. Then, watching the animated talk and the convivial atmosphere, one wonders if there is a better way to spend a vacation than en famille.

A FERRYBOAT TO THE GOOD LIFE

Above : On the pale gray and white veranda are comfortable chairs with armrests wide enough to hold a book or a plate.
Right : With its portico and turrets, the house evokes an old lighthouse.

$\mathcal{T}$he lawn slopes gently from a little knoll down to the water. Buttressed by a series of octagonally-shaped corners, accented by a tall flagpole, the house has the picturesque look of an old lighthouse. With its wings and gables and porches-full of wicker furniture and Adirondack chairs, impeccably arrayed, and its large glassed-in veranda where one can sit sheltered from the damp wind that blows in off the sea, it seems to be standing at attention. Everything here « feels so American », according to its owners, « so much a part of

160

our New England heritage. »

Stillness reigns. The only sounds are the twittering of birds in the trees, the hum of the lawn mower circling the pool and tennis court, and the sporadic drone of an outboard motor in the bay.

Shelter Island is reached by an antiquated little ferryboat that has been owned by the same family for generations, and unloads its cargos of cars and summer people like old friends every year. They come to renew themselves away from the tensions of New York City, and to relax in their elegantly eccentric houses dotted along the shore.

Adamantly resisting proposals to link their island to the mainland by a bridge, these residents set great store by their relative inaccessibility. With these families, many of the same ones returning year after year, Shelter Island is almost a self-contained community— and a good place to make friends that last a lifetime. The island feels like a piece of New England with its gently rolling hills—the perfect setting for long bike rides down breezy, tree-lined roads.

Every day is spent outdoors; in the early morning you can hear the screen doors banging as the kids run outside—perhaps to go swimming or « treasure hunting » along the beach. Later, they may have a picnic in the shadow of the boat house, or go biking with their friends, or set up a lemonade stand by the side of the road.

Meanwhile, their parents play tennis or sail, passing by one of the roadside stands on their way home to buy fresh corn, tomatoes, and other farm produce. As the sun goes down, everyone returns, glowing from the day's adventures, to sit on the porch in the golden light and share stories.

It is a revivifying change from city life, particularly for this couple, who each run a creative business in Manhattan. But there is still

Double preceding page :
A mosaic of flowers,
stripes, and old fabrics
for this summer living

room of wicker furniture.
Above : An
oval opening in
a wood trellis frames a
view of the dock.
Right : Against
a gray-shingled
wall, two chairs
brightened
by pastel touches.

164

entertaining to be planned: an all-day fishing trip from Mantauk perhaps, an evening cookout on the lawn, or a dinner party for friends and neighbors.

To help with this, two *au pair* girls are hired for a stay of two years. They become immersed in every aspect of the life of the family, learning the creative disciplines that make a summer house run smoothly.

So, when the table is set to perfection in the dining room, the lovely roses cut from the garden are softy lit by candles, and a green and yellow gazpacho is being served, the girls, for whom this experience has been a « rite of passage, » partake in its pleasures almost as much as the family and their guests.

Top left : In the old boat house, a Victorian pagoda bird cage and a few fond memories pinned to the wall. Above : Post cards and glasses made into candle holders. Following double pages : Under a nineteenth century map of the world, a still life with blue and white china. The play of sunlight and shadow through the circle of a Thai paper parasol. A relaxing moment on a bed covered with antique cretonne.

167

Resorts

At the end of the last century the aristocracy, with the haute bourgeoisie hot on its heels, discovered the benefits of bathing in the sea. This was the era of bathhouses on wheels being pulled to the water's edge by horses, and of fashionable ladies in hats and gloves, even on the beach. The crowned heads of Europe fanned the flames of this new rage. People flocked to Le Touquet in the wake of the Prince of Wales, and to Arcachon, which Emperor Napoleon III graced with his presence. Villas sprang up on oceanfronts everywhere. Baroque, ornamented with turrets, somewhere between neoGothic châteaux and Norman manors, their facades were arrayed in a kind of delirious mosaic along the coast. It was a brilliant time; people moved in for the summer to savor the exquisite leisure of life in these new seaside resorts.

In time, bourgeois traditions juxtaposed themselves with the worldly, aristocratic whirl. Families came to Le Touquet, to Arcachon and Dinard, inhaling together the intoxicating sea air that puts a sparkle in the eye. And while Panama hats may have given way to blue jeans, the sun-drenched days and the sailboat-dotted sea still remain as backdrops to long, happy summers on the shore.

A CENTURY OF SUMMERS

Above : Rising from a rocky point off Saint Malo, an immense granite villa typical of Breton architecture of the last century. Right : Standing on a folding wicker picnic chair, two cousins wait for their good night kiss.

*C*ertain country houses, by their very existence, heighten the pleasures of a vacation. A house named Saint-Germain is one of these. Rising above the Atlantic on the rocky tip of Moulinet Point, it is both a kind of lighthouse, watching over the entrance to Dinard harbor, and a symbol—a symbol because every summer since the turn of the century it has welcomed back a family that loves it and whose memories it safeguards.

« When

In the vestibule with its
walls of trompe l'oeil
stone, slickers, fishing nets,
and oars have been left on
the rustic nineteenth
century Breton chest
where boating gear is
kept. <u>Above</u> : A little girl
in a big straw hat looks at
herself in the mirrors of
the linen closet on the
second floor landing.

my grandfather bought this ugly stone pile he lost no time remodeling according to the prevailing taste, » his grandson Jérôme remembers. « The result : an enormous mansion with at least eighteen bedrooms and, as if that weren't enough, a sort of cottage that served as an annex, plus all kinds of mad structures scattered around the evergreen gardens that skirt the Point, with corridors of trees opening onto vistas of the sea. The children used to scare themselves to death hiding in this maze of green tunnels until it got dark. Today, they pitch their tents and sleep under the weltering trees, within earshot of the roar of the surf.

« Dotted with striped canvas cabanas, Dinard's beach lies in the cove between Moulinet and Malouine Points. In my grandfather's day,

<u>Left</u> : The children's dining room.
<u>Above</u> : The cozy living room.
<u>Right</u> : Making shell designs on a pie crust.

Above : On the vanilla-
colored paneling, a child's
portrait in red chalk.
Opposite : Blue accented
with green. On a
nineteenth century
bamboo dressing table,
souvenirs and seashells.
Right : One of the
bedrooms looks out on a
terrace bordered by a stone
balustrade. A nineteenth
century rattan chair ; an
American patchwork quilt
on the bed.

182

Above : The pine-paneled
childrens' rooms are all
named for places visible
from their windows. A
guest room with its big
Louis XVI bed. *Right :*
Dinard in bygone days
seen in an album of old
post cards.

we had wooden bathhouses for storing our collection of pails, shovels
and rakes. Now, the children only go down to the beach in the
afternoon, while we grown-ups swim in the morning. On the way
back, we stop at the cottage, which is almost always filled with
friends, and have a glass of white wine. Then, a little tipsily, our
bathrobed procession makes its way up to the main house where a
real lunch awaits. Meals are always served indoors, and there are
generally about fifteen of us at table.

« The afternoons are devoted to boating, an enjoyable but tricky
sport in these parts: the sea is often rough, the winds unreliable, the
tides huge, and there are rocks everywhere. One of our favorite
destinations is Cézembre Island, a famous landmark for gulls and

cormorants. We stagger ashore, exhausted but triumphant, having been drenched with spray several times on the way. Already soaked, we swim anyway; then settle down to a glass of wine and a bite of sausage.

« We always get home in time to see the sun set. From the terrace, we watch it hover above the horizon while a golden light floods the living room. That's when we all gather before dinner, relaxed, bathed and changed, and all in excellent moods.

« Evenings at Saint-Germain are delectably long and the talk is lively. The living room, with its English look and big alcove full of sofas and comfortable chairs, lends itself perfectly to conversation. And when we're not out on the water or talking together, we admire the sea. Between Saint-Malo and the Channel Islands, there is an endless parade of boats: ferryboats, yachts, and little sailboats, always entertaining.

« Today Saint Germain is the rallying point for the whole family. Except for the bedroom walls, which have been repainted, the decor has hardly changed at all.

« There are often thirty of us in residence, which means that shopping plays an important part in our lives: for groceries, of course, but also for flowers. Saint Germain is always full of flowers, and also full of friends, an open house where a constant flow of guests comes and goes.

« The soul of the house, the person without whom none of this would be possible, is Maman. So the big party of the summer always takes place on August 21, her birthday. Everyone makes sure they are there to join in this celebration; it's our way of honoring her and also thanking her for all she does to make our holidays so pleasant. »

*Left : Fishing for prawns
at high tide in Chausey.
Above : On the
mahogany sideboard,
lobsters, crabs and other
seafood are served on a set
of faïence plates ; each
plate shows a different
seascape. Opposite : On
the service counter,
mackerel and eel lie in
baskets lined with
seaweed.*

Resorts

Above : A pretty hair dressing table below an antique mirror. Opposite : In a large corner bedroom, a pine bedstead and skirted love seat, its cretonne print dating from the 1870's. Right : The ritual of the after-the-beach shower. Following double page : A little beach in a cove on the Ile d'Yeu.

188

INLET WITH HYDRANGEAS

Above : In the entryway outside the living room, seascapes, family portraits, books and a wood staircase fragrant from many waxings. Right : An English garden that slopes gently down to the sea.

A grass path leads to the sea, bordered by clumps of hydrangeas—flowers that are native to Brittany—and by camelias with glossy leaves. At the end of the path, with its look of a slightly windblown English garden, one comes to a little beach nestled in the curve of the bay.

It is a beautiful day. The countryside is haloed in blue light—not the dazzling, unbearably intense blue that transfixes the landscape in the Midi, but a transparent, faintly iridescent blue through which delicate grays are filtered, as changeable as the sea. However, in

192

*Double preceding page :
The timeless feeling of the
living room where
furniture and objects have
been collected over the
generations. To the right
and left of the fireplace,
two lacquered Dutch
sideboards one inlaid with
colored wood. Opposite :
The Baron Gudin, noted
during the Second Empire
for his seascapes painted
this portrait of one of his
daughters painted about
1825 .*

southern Brittany, one is never safe from the storms that come up suddenly, out of nowhere.

All at once it gets dark as night outside, and rain falls in sheets for a time. Then, the horizon clears and a new sky appears, washed clean of melancholy hues.

With its thick walls of rugged stone and its heavy slate roof, the house has weathered many summer and winter storms. Solidly moored in the Breton soil, it was built to withstand the onslaughts of nature as well as those of time.

Indoors, things have been accumulated over the generations. Rather old-fashioned canvases hang haphazardly on the walls: portraits of model little girls, of proud women in slightly tarnished gilt frames, and seascapes dating from the Second Empire, full of homely romanticism.

In the living and dining rooms, furniture and precious objects brought back by grandmothers, inveterate world travelers, form a sort of family puzzle.

But there are also comfortably sagging couches, piles of straw hats and baskets, and a deck chair that sits at the bottom of the brightly waxed staircase. There are books, too—the kinds of books one keeps and leafs through with pleasure, even when one is no longer the right age to read them.

This morning, an almost golden light streams in the windows. No one is home. The family has gone fishing, or to the village for the newspaper and a cup of coffee at the Bar de la Marine. They'll be back in time for lunch. Oysters, white wine, fresh bread and salted butter will be served, and they'll linger a while inside these stout gray walls, built to last forever.

Right : In a big house where one can enjoy both the garden and the sea, an entire room is devoted to collections of baskets that expand from year to year.

198

RETURN FROM THE COLONIES

*I*t was from the sailboat carrying him to Cap Ferret that the playwright Jean Anouilh first spotted his future summer house. White, and of colonial inspiration, it stood at the water's edge silhouetted against a cloudless blue sky.

Built in 1870 by English globe-trotters, it is a vast abode, with almost all its rooms facing the sea. Inside, an eclectic assemblage of battered Victorian armchairs, mahogany tables and odd chests cohabited in dusty somnolence, the pine-paneled walls hidden under layers of paint. With the arrival of the Anouilhs, the walls were scraped down to their original warm wood tones. After their first summer, Anouilh and his family were wedded to the house forever.

Every year, at the end of May, the family excitedly spills out of their two cars, the return trip not scheduled until October. It takes time to learn to enjoy the good life and besides, Anouilh worked here during the summer months. Many of his plays were written in a secluded cabin near the garden where he shut himself up every morning while the children had their swimming lesson.

« He was often gone the whole morning, » his wife remembers. « I would wait. Finally, he would appear in the doorway, a few sheets of paper in his hand, and have

Above : Model of a three-master. Right : Built at the end of the last century and surrounded by a double veranda, this colonial-style villa was one of the first to appear on Cap Ferret.

200

a glass of white wine as a pick-me-up.

« Sometimes actors arrived unexpectedly by sea. Anouilh would peer at them through his binoculars and run away! But then he'd come back and greet his guests with open arms.

« Anouilh protected but did not isolate himself. The house was often bursting at the seams, with theater people mainly, and the atmosphere was relaxed. Besides, there were the five children, and we always had to be available to them.»

Once, in summer, the Anouilhs gave a dinner party on the terrace. The children had bought fireworks for the occasion, which they set up on the rocks. What did it matter that the fuses wouldn't light? The important thing, then and now, was to have fun.

The dining room is flanked on one side by the billiard room (right), and on the other by the living room (above). Following double page : The pine-paneled wall, were painted white in the second floor bedrooms, along with some eighteenth century-style furniture.

A DISCREET CHARM

Above : A Parisian town house a step away from the beach.

Right : In the green living room with its toile de Jouy curtains, an 1880 billiard lamp with opaline shades illuminates a game of cards.

When summer comes, the family traditionally closes up its Paris town house and returns to the more temperate shores of Normandy. The household staff goes first to « open » the country house, actually more like a mansion near the Parc Monceau than a family villa.

Every year, the children are settled on the third floor in their pine-paneled rooms, while friends and relatives occupy the large bedrooms on the second floor. The stairway descends into a vast entrance hall, almost always deserted, perpetually in semidarkness,

206

*Far left : In the pink
bedroom, a detail of
a dressing table designed
in 1920. Opposite : The
large bedroom at the end
of the hall opens onto the
Moorish landing. The
walls are paneled in
pine ; some of the
furniture, also of pine,
was made for
the bedroom at the turn
of the century.*

209

The Moorish landing
with its stucco and
notched arches,
architectural touches added
by a grandfather smitten
with exoticism, is now a
game room.

with walls decorated with garlands of seaweed and shells.

The drawing rooms are immense and magnificent, with very high ceilings. One of them, the least formal, is entirely covered with toile de Jouy of the unusual green the sea takes on just before a storm, and is reserved for cards and parlor games. The dining room, gleaming from many waxings, has a reassuring country feeling. Here the grown-ups gather to savor hot prawns with coarse salt as the soft, slightly damp night air sweeps in through the large French doors opened wide onto the garden and the sea beyond.

In the grand old days of the sailing regattas that were held before 1918, fishermen as well as yachtsmen competed in the races. To celebrate the most important events, memorable garden parties were given at the house, attended by Trouville's sporting and fashionable society and their families. The regattas were the high point of the summer.

Otherwise, life was as regular as clockwork. When not fishing off the Black Rocks, the family spent the morning on the beach in front of the house. In the afternoon, the young people might play a few civilized sets of tennis with their friends, while the younger children rode around the beach in horse-drawn wagons. On nice days, a foursome might go all the way to Deauville for a game of golf.

At around five every afternoon, a sort of ritual ballet began on the boardwalk: strollers passing one another at a leisurely pace, and occasionally bowing. On the lawn, shaded by large pale umbrellas, the family took tea to the clinking of tiny spoons. The children's shining eyes would linger on the candy-colored macaroons...living memories for the present family.

Right : Slim columns decorated by an unknown artist support the arches of what must have been, at the turn of the century, a little oriental salon full of bric-a-brac.

Following double page : Gulls at rest near the quays.

BEACH GAMES AND GOOD MANNERS

*T*he move to Le Touquet for the season? It was a veritable military operation! » the present owner of the house remembers. « There were never less than eighteen people involved, not counting all the nannies and chambermaids and the cook—It was a way of life that demanded rigorous organization. Having servants required, for example, absolute punctuality for meals. Furthermore, it would never have crossed our minds to come to the table without having changed our clothes. Life on the beach was one thing, but the house was

216

Enormous villas, excessive yet comfortable like this one (above) built in 1926 by the architect Arsène Bical, sprang up along the waterfront. <u>Left</u> : Below them, an immense beach and bathhouses for changing.

With its paneling,
fireplace, books, antique
porcelain pharmaceutical
jars, 1930's leather club
chairs, the library, facing
the garden, is a warm
room where one detects a
certain English influence.
Opposite : In properly
run houses, every key has
its own label. *Right :* The
hall, with its ceramic tile
floor and dark,
oak-paneled walls.
On the Flemish table,
some Panama hats
for sunny days.

218

something else.

« In the summer, we always slept piled into one or two bedrooms. No one complained: we were having too good a time. Early in the morning, we would all tumble into the dining room for a hearty breakfast. Then, off to the beach. Since the weather in Le Touquet was unreliable, the regulars rented wooden cabanas in case of rain, usually one to a family. Every morning, our cabana arrived at the specified hour, pulled by a horse. We waited for it in front of the house, and told the driver where we wanted it taken.

Beside the wooden cabanas, brightly colored canvas tents were neatly lined up on the sand. I remember our shouts of laughter on very windy days, when the tents collapsed around the poor people

trying to change inside them! We often spent the entire day at the beach, digging tunnels and running in and out of the surf.

« But the main event of the summer was the sand castle competition. I prepared for it weeks in advance, storing up assorted shells and cuttlebones to decorate my future masterpiece. On the big day, the teams reported for work armed with pails, shovels and rakes. At the end of the afternoon, a benevolent jury went up and down the rows of fabulous creations. Once the winner had been announced, we lingered on the beach with the other contestants, comparing the merits of our ephemeral constructions until dinnertime when we rushed home, always terrified of being late for the evening meal.

Top left : The linen room, with its built-in cupboards full of sheets, antique tablecloths, and fine laces stored in cardboard boxes. _Below :_ One of the second-floor bedrooms with a wood and ceramic tile fireplace characteristic of the North. _Above :_ This hearty breakfast is served on a lace tablecloth from Boulogne.

Resorts

« Once every summer, following some mysterious annual tradition, my parents organized a picnic in the dunes—a perfect opportunity to do some sand sledding! Sometimes a windstorm would sneak up during lunch, and we would beat a hasty retreat, sandwich in hand, the wind whipping the backs of our legs. We would reach the house blown to bits, our mouths and eyes full of sand, and swearing we would never try that again.

« We whiled away the days among ourselves with not a care in the world, until suddenly, around August 15, the first flights of migratory birds would appear, skimming the waves in close formation. Their coming made us sad. We realized that fall was almost on our doorstep. »

Left : Above an imposing Breton sideboard laden with delicacies, antique Moustier and Lunéville plates are propped against wallpaper typical of the 1940's. Above left : In this truly traditional kitchen, a majestic coal stove presides. Right : On a damask tablecloth, a savory platter of shellfish. Following double page : Sail school.

Resorts

223

SUMMER IN THE WINTER CITY

*Above : A rock grotto
serves as a little theater for
the children.
Right : the imposing
Saint-Arnault villa, built
during the Second Empire.*

The Winter City in Arcachon is a maze of little streets lined with crooked houses. With its wooden balconies and stone facade, the villa Saint-Arnault looks like a Swiss chalet sitting atop a hill beside the sea.

Built by Field Marshal de Saint-Arnault in the mid-nineteenth century when the Pereire banking family was constructing entire neighborhoods, the villa Saint-Arnault is the complement to his summer residence, the villa de l'Alma, situated on the jetty in La Chapelle. In those days, no one would have dreamt of spending the winter beside the sea.

After the first storm, the Summer City closed its shutters and its inhabitants migrated 300 yards inland from the coast to their winter houses on the heights.

Today, nothing has changed very much in the region, and even less in the villa where time seems to have stood still.

It is July. Tintin tends the garden. Marthe busies herself in the kitchen. Both have been part of the house and of the family since—they can't even remember any more.

The children are coming! So many of them, with their parents and nannies. They'll unroll the spare mattresses, and the littlest ones will camp out in the dressing rooms off the grown-ups' bedrooms, and at the feet of the huge wooden grown-ups' beds, as big as Noah's arcs. The house feels right that way, when it is bursting at the seams.

At bedtime, much giggling and whispering, many cousinly secrets exchanged, and the sound of little bare feet racing down the stairs. Where is Maman? Sitting at the big table in the dining room with at least fifteen other people, as usual. Or perhaps she is already out on the porch where the grown-ups, a little cramped for space, always have their coffee and liqueurs.

At least they haven't left, as they do once a summer, to spend the evening at the Hôtel de la Plage. Then they're always gone such a long time.

They board the « Tot, » the family sailboat, and sail across the bay to the hotel, a simple little bistro surrounded by fishermen's cottages. It's always very late when they get home.

In the morning, at breakfast, plans for the day are hatched. There's the beach by the La Chapelle jetty, where the children usually go. Or they might walk to the ocean beach for a swim, and then have ice cream and waffles at the Cornet d'Amour.

Another vacation highpoint: picnics at the Banc d'Arghin, which happen according to an unvarying ritual. Departure is set for 11:00 in

Above : A family portrait.
Below : On a bamboo table, wooden napkin rings marked with each child's name. Right : The glassed-in winter porch, rattan furniture, couches upholstered in yellow canvas, and the famous Arcachon oysters.

228

Preceding page left : On the grand piano in the living room, little pastels and oils by an artist cousin are displayed. *Right :* From the villa's highest balcony, the view plunges to the Summer City, built beside the water. *Opposite :* Pastel toile de Jouy, lace bureau scarves, and eighteenth century-style furniture in a large sunny bedroom where nothing has changed since the villa was built.

Above, left : A newel post ornamented with a bevelled glass ball. Right : Beneath a neoclassic mirror, a nineteenth century porcelain wash basin. A Napoleon III ballroom chair. Right : This little girl will fall asleep in her bedroom, which is papered with tiny flowers. A Louis XVI chair painted gray. Last double page : A house marooned at high tide becomes accessible when the water recedes.

the morning. Parents, children and friends jam onto the « Tot » along with the eternal picnic basket, beach umbrellas, towels, shovels, buckets, life jackets, and the Gucci umbrella, constant companion of a favorite aunt. There is always some little kid who's lost his hat. After we land, we play games, and go swimming. Then we set the picnic out on a large tablecloth spread on the sand. The return trip is scheduled for six p.m., and we arrive back at the house as darkness falls, skin sticky with salt, dead tired, ecstatic.

As the days go by, beautiful summer turns to autumn when the villa Saint-Arnault will fall asleep again behind its closed shutters—until next year.

234

Acknowledgments

The author and the publisher wish to thank all those who have permitted their houses to be included in this book, houses which so beautifully exemplify the "spirit of family".

Hank Adams, Lindsay and Blake Allison, Sam, Morgan Allison, Mrs. Jean Anouilh, Mr. Nicolas Anouilh, Katie Anawalt Arnoldi and Charles Arnoldi, Mrs. Louis Balsan, Mr. and Mrs. Benoît Bartherotte, Princess of Bavière, Olivia Bell Buehl, Mr. and Mrs. Jean-Louis Bouscarle, Mr. Arnaud Bochand, Joan Bryan, Bandhany Bultman, Dan Carithers, Diane Carroll, Mrs. Geoffroy de Courcel, Mrs. Sylvie Delassus, Mrs. Maren Detering, Nikita and Bénédicte Droin, Mr. and Mrs. Maldwin Drummond, Stephen Ehrlich, Ray Ellis, Therese and George Elwell, Mr. Claude Fabry, Paula and Anthony Fisher, Candia Fisher, Tricia Foley, Erica and Peter Forbes, Mrs. de Fraiteur, James Corcoran Gallery, Kathryn George, Mr. and Mrs. Robert Gillet, Joseph Giovannini, Alison Greenberg, Marcia Grostein, Mrs. Jacqueline Hamm, Colombe and François d'Harcourt, Dave Hiller, Mr. and Mrs. Ernst Hirsch, Mrs. Kate Hunter, Hugh Newell Jacobsen, Joanne Jaffe, Mrs. Andrée Jaigu, Mr. and Mrs. Roderick James ("Seagull House", Dittisham, Mill Creek, Dartmouth, Devon), Eleanore and Michael Kennedy, Carol Klatt, Mr. and Mrs. Jean-Paul Le Pelley, Ruth Gardner Loew, Jim MacHugh, Cameron and Jeffrey MacKinley, Mrs. Nathalie de Maublanc, Mr. and Mrs. Jean-Louis Mellerio, Mr. and Mrs. Henri de Menton, Frank Miele, Mr. Yves Mousset, Mr. and Mrs. Jan Nordmark, Mr. and Mrs. Lindsay Owen-Jones, Max Palevsky, Mr. and Mrs. Pannet, Doctor Alexandre Patarot, Christine Pittel, Mrs. Nathalie Prouvost, Shyamoli and Taylor Pyne, Gary Rado, Barbara Nevin Realty, Mrs. Philippe Rohard, Barbara Rosenthal, Mr. and Mrs. Bernard Roux, Mr. and Mrs. Björn Sahlström, Charlotte Schoenfeld, Mrs. de Soussay, Sandy Carlson Tarlow and Richard Tarlow, Mrs. Thellier de Poncheville, Mrs. Ariane Turner-Laing, Viscountess Christina de Villoutreys, Mr. and Mrs. West Mac Cott.

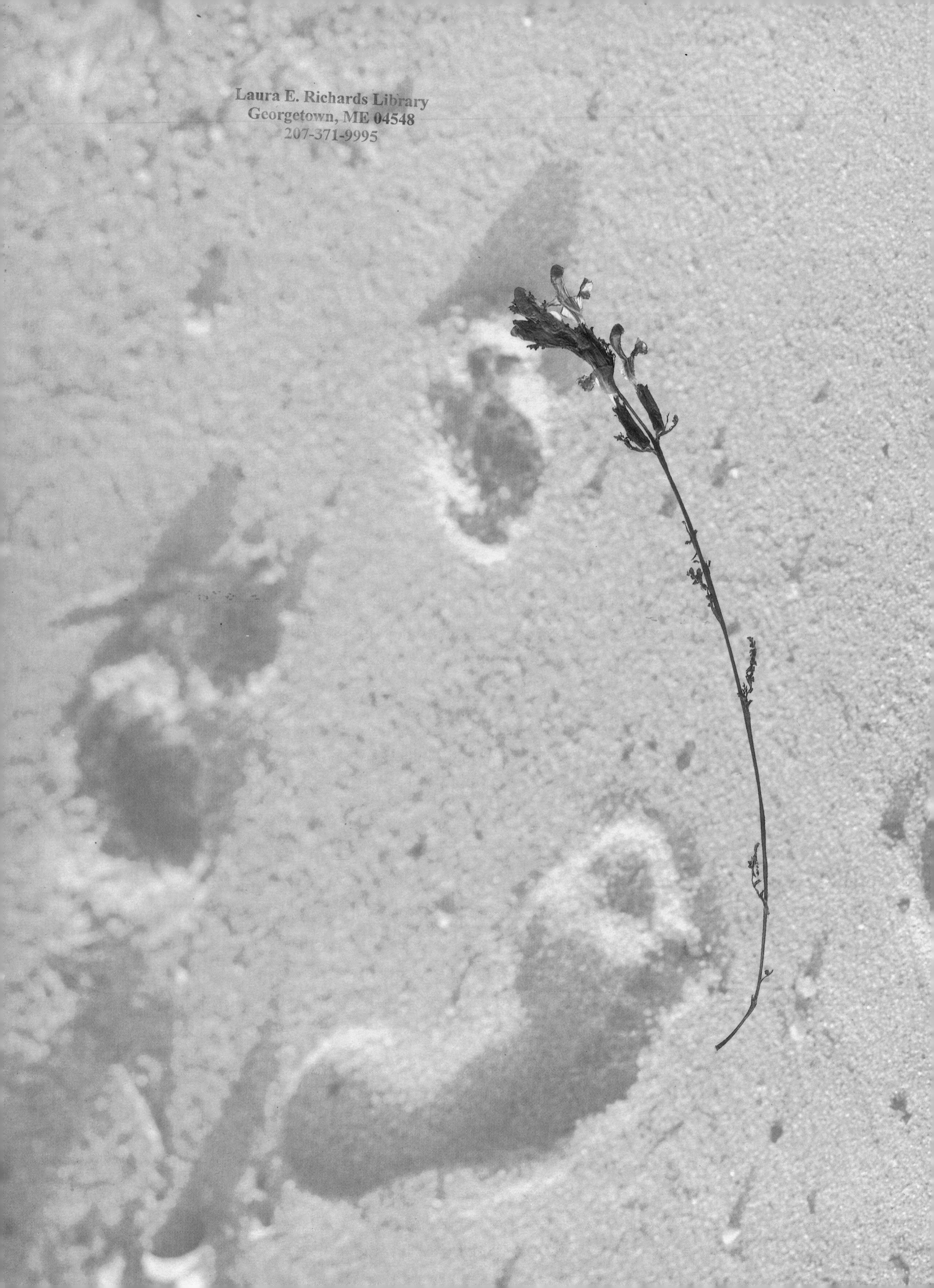